Mark A. Russo, CISSP-ISSAP

The National Institute of Standards and Technology (NIST) special publication series for federal cybersecurity only tell you "what to do." This series of supplements are designed to help you understand "how to" successfully implement the NIST 800-171 federal government contracting requirements.

NIST 800-171:
System Security Plan (SSP)
Template & Workbook
~ 2nd Edition

DEDICATION

This book is dedicated to the cyber-security men and women of the Department of Defense (DOD) and the United States Cybercommand (US Cybercommand) that protect and defend the Information Systems of this great Nation.

This is also dedicated to my family who have been supportive of my endeavors to plunge into writing as not just a hobby but a calling to make the world a better and more secure place.

Syber-Risk

NIST 800-171: System Security Plan Template & Workbook
by Mark A. Russo

January 2019: First Edition

Revision History for the First Edition
2019: First Release

On September 1, 2018 we launched the
Most Extensive Cybersecurity Blog Site

This is the major resource of everything "Cyber."
"The good, the bad, and the ugly of cybersecurity all in one place."

Join us at https://cybersentinel.tech

This free resource is available to everyone interested in the fate and future of cybersecurity in the 21st Century

NIST 800-171: System Security Plan (SSP) Template & Workbook

Table of Contents

What's on the Horizon? –Enforcement Actions

This is the 2019 update to the most popular book in the series addressing the challenges of NIST SP 800-171. Additional details are added in this version with expanded explanations of what each of the families are and how to best address them. This Second Edition is designed to help companies and agencies for the purposes of authorization with the federal government and more specifically the Department of Defense (DOD). This book can be used to review the 110 security controls, and provide a start point for a complete System Security Plan (SSP). An SSP fillable template is currently available at the site https://cybersentinel.tech.

A major 2019 NIST 800-171 development is the expected move by the Department of Justice (DOJ) against any company being held to either FAR Clause 52.204-21, DFARS Clause 252.204-7012, or both; if DOJ can show the company has violated its contract it will be subject to federal prosecution if they fail to meet NIST 800-171.

Discussions of the author with key personnel working with NIST and DOJ on this matter raises the seriousness of not meeting NIST 800-171. Sources to the author are expecting in 2019 and beyond the likelihood of civil and criminal prosecution for those companies who: 1) have a breach of their IT environment, 2) that data, specifically Controlled Unclassified Information (CUI)/Critical Defense Information (CDI), is damaged or stolen, and the 3) DOJ can demonstrate negligence by the company, will result in federal prosecution.

This is no longer a threat, but an actual development from within the federal government.

This development highlights some of the author's past concerns that companies should be hiring third-party assessors to review their SSP, their Plan of Action and Milestones (POAM) and company cybersecurity policies. While this will not completely absolve the company from prosecution, it may help reduce the company's liability to the federal government. If a breach occurs, the use of third-party assessors is one of many ways that companies can show "adequate security" measures were in place prior to the breach. This would demonstrate the company attempted to have third-party professionals help and assess the state of their IT environment.

This recommendation is even more vital as the federal government begins its likely 2019 course to hold companies accountable; showing more due diligence on the part of the company's cybersecurity effort _has become even for vital._

NIST 800-171: System Security Plan (SSP) Template & Workbook

An Introduction

There are **110** explicit security controls from NIST 800-171, revision 1, extracted from NIST's core cybersecurity document, NIST 800-53, *Security and Privacy Controls for Federal Information Systems and Organizations*, that are considered vital. This is a highly pared down set of controls for the purposes of Industry's requirements to meet federal government cybersecurity contracting requirements. There are over 800 potential controls offered from NIST 800-53 revision 4; this more expansive set of controls is used extensively by DOD to protect its IT systems from its jet-fighters to its vast personnel databases.

This SSP is based upon the NIST and National Archives and Records Administration (NARA) templates and provides a greater clarification to the company or agency representative, business owner, and their IT staff. This book is intended to focus business owners and their IT support staff on what is required to create and complete a **System Security Plan** (SSP) that sufficiently meets the NIST 800-171, revision 1, requirements. Companies need to focus on a "good faith" effort on how to best address these controls to the government—and, it more importantly will help the business protect its own sensitive data and Intellectual Property (IP).

In addition, the **People, Process and Technology (PPT) Model** is the recommended guidance for answering and responding to the controls within NIST 800-171. While all solutions will not require a **technological** answer, consideration of the **people** (e.g., who? what skill sets? etc.) and **process** (e.g., notifications to senior management, action workflows, etc.) will meet many of the response requirements. The best responses will typically include the types and kinds of people assigned to oversee the control, the process or procedures that identify the workflow that will ensure that the control is met, and in many cases, the technology that will answer the control in part or in full. (See Module #5 at Udemy.com for a free video describing the PPT Model at https://www.udemy.com/system-security-plan-ssp-for-nist-800-171-compliance/. Also, see the Access Control (AC) section below that provides three examples for you and your IT staff).

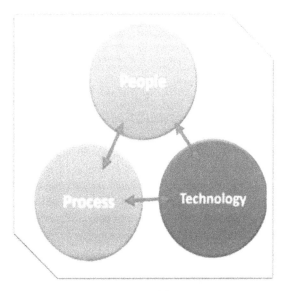

PPT Model

Expectations

In 2019, the expectation is that the United States (US) federal government will expand the National Institute of Standards and Technology (NIST) Special Publication (SP) 800-171, revision 1, **Protecting Unclassified Information in Nonfederal Information Systems and Organizations** cybersecurity technical publication will apply to the entirety of the federal government. It will require that any company, business, or agency, supporting the US Government is fully compliant with NIST 800-171 no later than the date of contract award.

The Federal Acquisition Regulation (FAR) Committee's Case # 2017-016 had an original suspense date of March 2018; that date has come and gone. The latest and expected timeframe for any final decision has moved to an expected timeframe now of "sometime in 2019."[1] While it is likely that the Federal Acquisition Regulation (FAR) Committee may further delay NIST 800-171 implementation, the value and the purpose of this book is no less critical.

Furthermore, while NIST 800-series Cybersecurity publications tell a business "what" is required, they do not necessarily help in telling "how" to meet the 110 security control requirements in NIST 800-171. The number of security controls may further increase based upon the actual or perceived threats to a federal agency. Companies should confirm control requirements with their respective Contract Office.

This book is created to help the small and big business owner in meeting the newest cybersecurity contracting requirement. It is intended to assist companies and their Information Technology (IT) staffs' on how to best address the challenges of meeting the 2016 National Institute of Standards and Technology (NIST) 800-171, revision 1. This further includes compliance with the Federal Acquisition Regulation (FAR) clause 52.204-21 and its companion DOD supplement, the Defense Federal Acquisition Regulation Supplement (DFARS), and its specific clause, 252.204-7012.

Additionally, this book is dedicated and created to give businesses and their IT staffs a substantive start-point. It is designed to walk through the security controls in enough detail to ensure authorization to operate and conduct regular business, goods and services, with the US federal government. This approach is offered in likely anticipation of a federal-wide requirement for all businesses attempting to show a "good-faith" representation of meeting the new NIST 800-171 requirements.

NIST 800-171 applies to **prime and subcontractors**. There are three core contractual obligations:

1. "Adequately safeguard" Controlled Unclassified Information (CUI), and if working with the Department of Defense (DOD), Covered/Critical Defense Information

---

[1] In the first edition, we anticipated late 2018. That final recommendation has still not occurred, but NIST 800-171 has had increasing emphasis in DOD and Department of Education; it may no longer be a critical decision point for NIST 800-171 implementation.

(CDI).

2. Provide timely cyber-incident reporting to the government when a IT network breach is identified; typically, within 72 hours or sooner.

3. If operating with a Cloud Service Provider (CSP), "adequate" security needs to be demonstrated; usually through a contract with the CSP that shows that they are providing adequate security to provide data protection as a third-party service provider. A contract or Service Level Agreement (SLA) should show the business is executing sound cybersecurity diligence to government Contract Officers (CO).

Also, see this book on how to prepare an effective Cloud Service Level Agreement (CSLA) on Amazon. Plan your SLA especially if considering a cloud storage solution for all or part of the business.

CLOUD SOLUTIONS BEGIN WITH A WELL-DESIGNED CLOUD SERVICE LEVEL AGREEMENT (CSLA)
This book is not another Cloud Security Theory book, it is a practical and how-to volume for both the Cloud Service Customer (CSC) and Cloud Service Provider (CSP) negotiate the CSLA based on defined terms and metrics. This is more than a high-level description of "risks and challenges" involved in entering a true CSLA. It is a "down in the weeds" approach with nearly 100 specific Service Level Objectives (SLO)—the next level down-- with suggested metrics that get you started on Day 1.

So you have decided to deploy part or all your business into a major cloud vendor. The questions are: 1) Will I get the functionality my business requires, and 2) more importantly, how do I know how secure it really is? This book is written to help you and your IT staff develop, review, and oversee an effective cloud implementation. We provide you with a large and detailed amount of Service Level Objectives (SLO) that ensure a smooth transition, and ultimately the framework to maintain a proper quality assurance and oversight mission. This book is based upon both US and international lessons learned and best practices designed to provide the value and return on investment that businesses rightfully demand.

What is "adequate security?" **Adequate security** is defined by "compliance" with the 110 NIST 800-171 security controls, and when the business is issued the solicitation, i.e., contract award. It will also be considered adequate upon an authorization issued to the business or company by the designated CO. This does not mean all security controls are in effect, but where a deviation is needed, a Plan of Action and Milestones (POAM) is provided.

A POAM is required as part of the official submission package to the government. It should identify why the company cannot currently address the control, and when it expects to resolve the control.

The business is also required to provide timely cyber-incident reporting to the government when a breach into its network has occurred. The DOD requirement, for example, is that the business notifies the government within 72 hours upon *recognition* of a security incident. (See the chapter on the Incident Response (IR) control family).

Additionally, the US Government may require the business to notify cybersecurity support and response elements within the federal government. This may include the Department of Homeland Security's (DHS) US Computer Emergency Response Team (US-CERT) (https://www.us-cert.gov/) or other like agency within the government.

Changing federal cybersecurity contract requirements are also taking into consideration the vast moves within the public and private sectors into cloud services. Typically, the security protections would be found in any contracts or SLA between the business and the CSP. These are normally sufficient evidence for the government.

The good news regarding CSPs are there are many current CSPs that are already in compliance with the government's Federal Risk and Authorization Management Program (FedRAMP). Being FEDRAMP-compliant prior to final submission of the NIST 800-171 Body of Evidence (BOE) will reduce the challenges of using an uncertified CSP; plan accordingly if considering moving part or all the business' operations into the "cloud."

Consequences of Non-compliance

There are several major consequences contractors and their subcontractors need to consider if either unable to meet or maintain their compliance. This can include several serious consequences and it is vital the business stays current regarding any changes in their cybersecurity posture. Stay constantly current regarding any new NIST 800-171 direction in general, or specific to the agency being supported. Failing to stay current with the Contract office may jeopardize business relationships with the government. These consequences may include:

- Impact to Future Contract Selection. This may be as basic as a temporary disbarment from federal contract work. It could also include permanent measures by government to suspend a company for a much longer period. Furthermore, the government could pursue the company for fraud or clear misrepresentation of their security posture to the US Government. This most likely would occur when a cybersecurity **incident** occurs within the businesses' network. This most likely would result in government appointed third-party assessor that would determine whether there was a willful disregard for NIST 800-171 and any associated FAR/DFARS clauses. *Remember*, the business will always be assessed against the following criteria:
  - Was there **adequate security** in place prior and during the incident?
  - Were the protections adequately established based upon a **good-faith** effort by the company to protect CUI/CDI?

- Assessments Initiated by the Government. At this phase, the Government will have unfettered access to determine culpability of the incident and whether it further brought harm against the government and its agencies. Cooperation is a key obligation and hiding the incident may have worse impacts than not reporting the intrusion.

- A POAM will be required. The government will most likely mandate a POAM be developed to address the finding. This should be a good effort to identify interim milestones with final and planned completion dates to ensure a situation will not reoccur. (See the supplement: *Writing an Effective Plan of Action & Milestones*: https://www.amazon.com/Writing-Effective-Plan-Action-Milestones-

ebook/dp/B07H2M3F2M/ref=sr_1_2?ie=UTF8&qid=1536967628&sr=8-
2&keywords=POAM)

- **Loss of Contract.** Worse case, the Contract Officer may determine that the company failed to meet the cybersecurity requirements. The results of that determination most likely will result in cancelation of the contract for *cause*.

The Likely Course: FAR Clause 52.204-21

For <u>very basic</u> safeguarding of contractor information systems that process, store, or transmit federal "contract information," expect this clause will be modified to reduce several of the specific NIST 800-171 security controls. A pared down selection of controls would be used in the early stages of NIST 800-171 implementation and transition for a federal agency. FAR 52.204-21 may be modified to about fifteen (15) "basic" cybersecurity controls for the contractor's information system. This will apply most typically to "federal contract information" where a company clearly stores, processes or transmits federal data. The specific language is:

> *"Information, not intended for public release, that is provided by or generated for the Government under a contract to develop or deliver a product or service to the Government, but not including information provided to the public (such as on public Web sites) or simple transactional information, such as necessary to process payments."*

This clause will <u>not</u> require all 110 security controls and is expected to reduce or minimize the following types of associated controls:
1) Cybersecurity training requirements
2) Two-factor authentication (2FA)
3) Detailed system control descriptions
4) Cybersecurity incidents or breach notifications

Expect few federal agencies to apply this clause long-term since it opens the federal agency to both public and congressional scrutiny. Expect this to be applied as a short-term solution until such time a future contract modification occurs, and the agency is more confident in its understanding and application of NIST 800-171.

Finally, this book is still applicable for FAR 52.204-21 implementation scenario. It can be used to answer the expected 15 security controls as identified in subsequent chapters of this book. Verify the actual required security controls with the Contract Office. It is important to confirm the needed control explanations as described later in the specified in later chapters and their respective control family.

Minimum proof of Cybersecurity Posture

The basis of NIST 800-171 is that contractors provide adequate security on all covered contractor Information Systems (IS). Typically, the minimum requirement to demonstrate control implementation is through **documentation**. Another term that is used is an **artifact**. An artifact is any representation to an independent third-party assessor that clearly shows compliance with a specific security control. It is a major part of the proof that a business owner would provide to DOD or other federal government contract office.

The common term for the collection of all applicable and supporting artifacts is the Body of Evidence (BOE). The major items required for the BOE includes three major items:

1. **System Security Plan (SSP).** This is a standard cybersecurity document. It describes the company's overall IT infrastructure to include hardware and software lists. Where appropriate, suggestions of additional artifacts that should be included in this document and duplicated into a the standard SSP format will be recommended. The current generalized direction for the SSP is the current minimum requirement for an artifact and must also include all Plans of Actions and Milestones (POAM); the POAM is not addressed in full for the purposes of this supplement and is considered a separate artifact.

2. **Plans of Action and Milestones (POAM).** This describes any control that the company cannot fix or fully demonstrate its full compliance. It provides an opportunity for a company to delay addressing a difficult to implement technical solution or in many cases may be cost-prohibitive. (See upcoming supplement *NIST 800-171: Writing an Effective POAM on Amazon*).

   Furthermore, POAMs should always have an expected completion date and defined interim milestones (typically monthly) that describe the actions leading to a full resolution or implementation of the control. *POAMs should not be for more than a year, however, a critical hint, a company may request an <u>extension</u> multiple times if unable to fully meet the control.*

3. **Company Policy** or **Procedure.** Any corporate direction provided to internal employees, subcontractors, and some third-party service providers such as Managed or Cloud Service Providers. This direction is typically enforceable under United States labor laws and Human Resource (HR) direction. It is recommended that such a policy or procedure artifact be a *singular* collection of how the company addresses each of the 110 security controls.

REMINDER: All policy or procedure requirements are best captured in a single business policy or procedure guide. This should address the controls aligned with the security control families

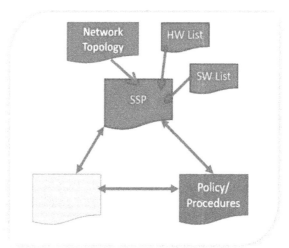

The Major Artifacts Required by the Federal Government under NIST 800-171

When working with the government simple and consistent always helps through a very young and less-than-defined process

POAMs must be Defined Well

The POAM is used where the business cannot meet or address the control either for technical reasons, "we don't have a Data at Rest (DAR) encryption program," or cost, "we plan to purchase the DAR solution No Later Than April 1, 2019." POAMs should include **milestones**;

milestones should describe what will be accomplished over time to prepare for the full implementation of the control in the future. What will the business do in the interim to address the control? This could include, for example, other **mitigation** responses of using improved physical security controls, such as a 24-7 guard force, the addition of a steel-door to prevent entry to the main computer servers, or improved policies that have explicit repercussions upon company personnel.

POAMs will always have a defined end date. Typically, it is either within 90 days, 6 months, or a year in length. For DOD, one year should be the maximum date; however, the business, as part of this fledgling process can request an extension to the POAM past the "planned" end date. RMF affords such flexibilities; don't be afraid to exercise them as appropriate.

A CRITICAL NOTE ABOUT POAM SECURITY

How important is it to protect your POAM? It is critical that your vulnerabilities are controlled and only released to personnel who require access to the information. If the POAM listing were to become public, would-be hackers would have an easy "blueprint" of how to exploit the IT infrastructure. POAM information should always be treated as highly sensitive and the sharing of it should only be with those with a clear need-to-know. Always treat POAM information as information that should be secured in at least lockable and restricted areas both in its hard copy as well as softcopy online form.

[bracketed italicized paragraphs provide additional information on how to best approach the question or situation within an official SSP]

All downloadable and fillable templates for this book are NOW available at: https://cybersentinel.tech.

*** Check out the Cyber-Shop*

**CONTROLLED UNCLASSIFIED INFORMATION (CUI)/
CRITICAL DEFENSE INFORMATION (CDI)[2]
[when filled in for ALL pages]**

COMPANY LOGO HERE

System Security Plan (SSP) [Template]
[SYSTEM NAME "Company A Information System"> <VERSION "(1.0)"]

Report Prepared By	<Name/position>
Date of Original SSP	<Initial Submission>
Date of Latest SSP Update	<Date>

---

[2] Security markings are based on DOD standards or at the direction of the Contract Office. Non-DOD agencies should only be marked CUI. As always, confirm all security markings from your respective Contract Office.

CHANGE RECORD

Date	Description	Editor:

Background

This **System Security Plan** (SSP) is provided to meet requirements under the National Institute of Standards and Technology (NIST) Special Publication (SP) 800-171 version 1, *Protecting Controlled Unclassified Information in Nonfederal Systems and Organizations,* and the Risk Management Framework (RMF). Compliance is in accordance with applicable Federal Acquisition Regulation (FAR) and [if not a DOD contractor delete 'DFARS' portion following] Defense Federal Acquisition Regulation Supplement (DFARS) 252.204-7012 clauses. It applies to Nonfederal System Owners (NSO) and Organizations conducting business with the US Government. It applies to Information Systems (IS) to include Local Area Networks, Wide Area Networks and Interconnected Systems used in the conduct of authorized business activities with the federal government.

Applicability

The SSP is applicable to all Information Systems (IS) that store, process and/or transmit Controlled Unclassified Information (CUI)/Covered Defense Information (CDI) [for DOD contractors only] specific to NIST SP 800-171, rev 1, and any directed updates as found in the NARA CUI Registry.

---

1. SYSTEM IDENTIFICATION

1.1. System Name/Title: *[State the name of the system. Spell out acronyms. This could be as basic as "Company 'A' Information System," or "Company 'B' "Sunflower" Inventory System Database"].*

1.1.1. System Categorization: <u>Moderate for Confidentiality</u>

> ***1.1.1.1.*** *[Confidentiality=MODERATE, Integrity and Availability are not required at this time to be categorized either by the Government or the business, respectively.*

> ***1.1.1.2.*** *This is describing that your IT system is complying with the 'moderate' security controls; this is the current standard categorization for all IS's required to comply with NIST 800-171]*

1.1.2. System Unique Identifier: *[Insert any System Unique Identifier; this will be how the DOD or Federal Agency identifies the business system for "reporting" purposes.]*

1.1.3. Responsible Organization: *[Company CEO, President, or Facility Security Officer (FSO)]*

Name:	
Address:	
Phone:	

1.1.4 Information Owner: *[Government POC responsible for providing and/or receiving CUI; this typically should be the designated Contract Officer Representative (COR) or assigned Contract Specialist]:*

Name:	
Title:	
Office Address:	
Work Phone:	
e-Mail Address:	

1.1.5 System Owner: *[This should be a senior company officer, the assigned Chief Information Officer (CIO), or IT Program Manager responsible for managing the company's IT infrastructure.]:*

Name:	
Title:	
Office Address:	
Work Phone:	
e-Mail Address:	

1.1.6 **System Security Officer:** *[This would be typically the Information System Security Officer/Engineer (ISSO/E or Chief Information Security Officer (CISO))]:*

Name:	
Title:	
Office Address:	
Work Phone:	
e-Mail Address:	

1.2 **General Description/Purpose of System:** *[What is the function/purpose of the system? Provide a brief description of your security environment and kinds of services it provides. This could, for example, include logistics ordering, personnel records storage, or financial services. This description will help the company or agency identify what is determined as being CUI/CDI or not.]*

_____

_____

_____

1.2.3 Number of end users and privileged users: *[Provide the <u>approximate</u> number of users and administrators of the system. Include those with privileged access such as system administrators, database administrators, application administrators, etc. Add rows to define different roles as needed.]*

User Roles and Number of Each Type

Overall User Numbers	Number of Administrators/ Privileged Users with Elevated Privileges

1.2.4 General Description of Information:

1.2.4.1 *[CUI/CDI information types processed, stored, or transmitted by the system are determined and documented. For more information, see the **CUI Registry** at https://www.archives.gov/cui/registry/category-list.] This will describe the types and kinds of situations when the documents, either soft or hard copy, must be properly marked and protected.*

1.2.4.2 *Typically, DOD or the respective federal agency will provide documents that are marked based upon the CUI Registry requirements. For further clarification, it is always best to document your requests for interpretation to the assigned Contracting Officer or his designated representative.*

1.2.4.3 *Document the CUI/CDI information types processed, stored, or transmitted by the system below].*

_____

_____

_____

2. SYSTEM ENVIRONMENT

2.1 Physical Network Topology:

2.1.1 (See Module 3 for SSP on Udemy.com at https://www.udemy.com/system-security-plan-ssp-for-nist-800-171-compliance/ **)**

2.1.2 [Include a <u>detailed physical</u> topology narrative and graphic that clearly depicts the system boundaries, system interconnections, and key devices. (Note: this does not require depicting every workstation or desktop, but include an instance for each operating system in use, an instance for portable components (if applicable), all virtual and physical servers (e.g., file, print, web, database, application), as well as any networked workstations (e.g., Unix, Windows, Mac, Linux), firewalls, routers, switches, copiers, printers, lab equipment, handhelds).

2.1.3 If components of other systems that interconnect/interface with this system need to be shown on the diagram, denote the system boundaries by referencing the security plans or names and owners of the other system(s) in the diagram.

2.1.4 Insert a system topology graphic. Provide a narrative consistent with the diagram that clearly lists and describes each system component.]

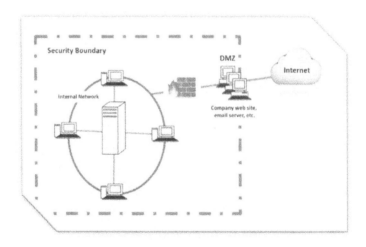

Example Physical Network Topology Diagram

2.2 Hardware Listing

2.1.5 **(See Udemy.com** https://www.udemy.com/system-security-plan-ssp-for-nist-800-171-compliance/ **)**

2.1.6   *[Include or reference a complete and accurate listing of all hardware (a reference to the organizational component inventory database is acceptable) and software (system software and application software) components, including make/OEM, model, version, service packs, and person or role responsible for the component.]*

2.1.7   **See Appendix A – Hardware Listing**

2.1.7.1   *[You can obtain this template at https://cybersentinel.tech]*

2.1.8   Software Listing

2.1.8   **See Appendix B – Software Listing**

2.1.8.1   *[You can obtain this template at https://cybersentinel.tech]*

2.2 **Hardware and Software Maintenance and Ownership** – [Is all hardware and software maintained and owned by the organization? This should address any third-party maintenance support to include Managed (external) or Cloud Service Providers(CSP).

2.2.1   *[Refer to NIST 800-171 Maintenance (MA) control discussed below. See the publication: **NIST 800-171: Beyond DOD** on Amazon for a detailed discussion.*

2.2.2   *If no, explain how maintenance for IS hardware and software components are generally maintained.]*

_____

_____

_____

_____

3. REQUIREMENTS

3.1 The source of these requirements is derived from the 2016 National Institute of Standards and Technology (NIST) Special Publication (SP) 800-171, revision 1, ***Protecting Controlled Unclassified Information in Nonfederal Information Systems and Organizations;*** *ensure that* *you are working from the 2016 Revision 1 version.*

3.2 Provide a thorough description of how all the security requirements are being implemented or planned to be implemented. The description for each security requirement contains:

1) The security requirement number and description.

2) How the security requirement is being implemented or planned to be implemented based upon the **PPT Model** as suggested in the "examples" below.

3) Any **compensating mitigations**(s) in place due to implementation constraints in lieu of the stated requirement. This may include, for example, physical security controls designed to provide specific reinforcing actions for the control or other technological solution that provides partial abilities to reduce the risk based upon this technology.

4) If the requirement is **'Not Applicable'** to the system, provide rationale that technically identifies why this control has no basis for being reviewed/assessed; this could include, for example, the application of any Wi-fi controls where the technical environment either does not have or does not allow it within the current security architecture.

ID	FAMILY	ID	FAMILY
AC	Access Control	MP	Media Protection
AT	Awareness and Training	PE	Physical and Environmental Protection
AU	Audit and Accountability	PL	Planning
CA	Security Assessment and Authorization	PS	Personnel Security
CM	Configuration Management	RA	Risk Assessment
CP	Contingency Planning	SA	System and Services Acquisition
IA	Identification and Authentication	SC	System and Communications Protection
IR	Incident Response	SI	System and Information Integrity
MA	Maintenance	PM	Program Management

NIST 800-171 Security Control Identifiers and Family Names

Access Control (AC)

Access Control (AC) is probably the most technical and most vital security control family within the cybersecurity process. It is designed to focus computer support personnel, System Administrators (SA), or similar IT staff, on the technical security protections of critical data. This will include any CUI/CDI and internal sensitive data maintained by the company's IT infrastructure and maintained by the company as part of doing business with the government. If making investments in cybersecurity infrastructure upgrades, the *AC control will provide the greatest Return on Investment.*

Also, it is important to confirm whether either a technical solution is not already embedded in the current IT system. Many times, controls are ignored, captured by policy, or a POAM is developed, even though some base capabilities to address the control are already resident in the base system or more particularly within the network Operating System (OS). Also, check for accessory applications provided by the OS manufacturer to determine whether a no-cost solution is already resident. Ask the IT staff to confirm whether there is an existing technical solution as part of the system to avoid spending additional dollars for capabilities already in place.

Where cost is currently prohibitive to implement, a POAM is an acceptable but temporary solution. If unable to address the control during the company's "self-assessment" effort, then be prepared to formulate a Plans of Action and Milestone (POAM). (*Writing an Effective POAM* is a current supplement to this book on Amazon®).

3.1.1 Limit system access to authorized users, processes acting on behalf of authorized users, and devices (including other systems).

☐ Implemented   ☐ Not Implemented - Planned - Requires POAM   ☐ Not Applicable

INSTRUCTIONS: Is the control fully 'Implemented'? If the control is 'planned to be implemented' a Plan of Action and Milestone (POAM) will be required. If "Not Applicable," provide a technical rationale why the control does not apply to the IT company's IT environment.

This should describe how the control is being implemented. You should also reference where in either the SSP or a Company policy or procedure guide where the control is addressed. Assume this information is subject to audit/assessment by the Contract Office.

EXAMPLE #1: PPT Model:

1. *People: "The Company Cybersecurity procedure guide addresses the differences between the general and privileged users. Privileged users, having elevated privileges and potential "super-user" access for other users will be limited to specified IT personnel with requisite responsibilities to manage the network, and have the appropriate training.*

3. *Process: Those with elevated privileges will have, at a minimum, been appointed in writing by the Chief Information Officer (CIO) and have completed Operating System training specific to the company's current IT environment.*

4. *Technology: The company uses the Cyberark® product to further audit those with privileged access, and that information is provided to the CIO weekly."*

_____

_____

_____

_____

3.1.2 Limit system access to the types of transactions and functions that authorized users are permitted to execute.

☐ Implemented   ☐ Not Implemented -   ☐ Not Applicable
                              Planned - Requires POAM

EXAMPLE #2: PPT Model:

1. *People (general user): "This control will be addressed in the business policy/procedural document. General users are only authorized "basic" access to the company's IS system; this includes electronic mail, Internet access, and the Microsoft® business products purchased for the explicit purpose of conducting their daily duties as part of their functions to support business goals and objectives.*

2. *Process: They may not add or remove applications without following submitting a "Change Request" form developed by the Office of the CIO and verified by their 1ˢᵗ line supervisor and approved by the Deputy CIO for Business Operations.*

3. *Technology: The use of Bitlocker® to enforce unenforced actions will be used to both "whitelist" authorized programs and functions, and "blacklist" all unauthorized sites such as gambling, pornography, etc., will be blocked.*

4. *People (privileged user): Those with privileged access which includes, for example, back-office maintenance, network care, account creation, database maintenance, etc. will be limited to only those functions a part of their duties; these duties will align with the privileged users' job*

description for the current year.

5. Process: Privileged user access reviews will be reassessed every year. Their access will be segregated by different logins and passwords for audit purposes.

6. Technology: The company uses the Cyberark® product to further audit those with privileged access, and the audit logs will be provided to the CIO weekly."

_____

_____

_____

_____

3.1.3 Control the flow of CUI in accordance with approved authorizations.

☐ Implemented   ☐ Not Implemented -   ☐ Not Applicable
                          Planned - Requires POAM

EXAMPLE #3: PPT Model:

1. People: "The company Cybersecurity procedure guide addresses that all users are required to apply built-in email encryption when transmitting CUI/CDI.

2. Process: The company uses flow control to manage the movement of CUI/CDI throughout the IT architecture; flow control is based on the types of information. Additional procedural concerns will be addressed: 1) Only authorized personnel within the company with the requisite need-to-know are provided access; 2) All Data in Transit (DIT) will be encrypted using at a minimum the Advanced Encryption Standard (AES) 256-bit key length encryption.

3. Technology: The company uses the ABC Company Advanced Encryption Standard (AES) 256-bit key length encryption application; only this product will be used for transiting CUI/CDI."

_____

_____

_____

_____

3.1.4 Separate the duties of individuals to reduce the risk of malevolent activity without collusion.

☐ Implemented   ☐ Not Implemented -   ☐ Not Applicable
Planned - Requires POAM

_____

_____

_____

_____

3.1.5 Employ the principle of least privilege, including for specific security functions and privileged accounts.

☐ Implemented   ☐ Not Implemented -   ☐ Not Applicable
Planned - Requires POAM

_____

_____

_____

3.1.6 Use non-privileged accounts or roles when accessing nonsecurity functions.

☐ Implemented   ☐ Not Implemented -   ☐ Not Applicable
Planned - Requires POAM

_____

_____

_____

_____

3.1.7 Prevent non-privileged users from executing privileged functions and audit the execution of such functions.

☐ Implemented   ☐ Not Implemented -   ☐ Not Applicable
                         Planned - Requires POAM

_____

_____

_____

_____

3.1.8 Limit unsuccessful logon attempts.

☐ Implemented   ☐ Not Implemented -   ☐ Not Applicable
                         Planned - Requires POAM

_____

_____

_____

_____

3.1.9 Provide privacy and security notices consistent with applicable CUI rules.

☐ Implemented   ☐ Not Implemented -   ☐ Not Applicable
                         Planned - Requires POAM

_____

_____

_____

_____

3.1.10 Use session lock with pattern-hiding displays to prevent access and viewing of data after period of inactivity.

☐ Implemented   ☐ Not Implemented -   ☐ Not Applicable
                    Planned - Requires POAM

_____

_____

_____

_____

3.1.11 Terminate (automatically) a user session after a defined condition.

☐ Implemented   ☐ Not Implemented -   ☐ Not Applicable
                    Planned - Requires POAM

_____

_____

_____

_____

3.1.12 Monitor and control remote access sessions.

☐ Implemented   ☐ Not Implemented -   ☐ Not Applicable
                    Planned - Requires POAM

_____

_____

3.1.13 Employ cryptographic mechanisms to protect the confidentiality of remote access sessions.

☐ Implemented   ☐ Not Implemented -   ☐ Not Applicable
                          Planned - Requires POAM

3.1.14 Route remote access via managed access control points.

☐ Implemented   ☐ Not Implemented -   ☐ Not Applicable
                          Planned - Requires POAM

3.1.15 Authorize remote execution of privileged commands and remote access to security-relevant information.

☐ Implemented   ☐ Not Implemented -   ☐ Not Applicable
                          Planned - Requires POAM

_____

_____

3.1.16 Authorize wireless access prior to allowing such connections.

☐ Implemented   ☐ Not Implemented -   ☐ Not Applicable
                         Planned - Requires POAM

_____

_____

_____

_____

3.1.17 Protect wireless access using authentication and encryption.

☐ Implemented   ☐ Not Implemented -   ☐ Not Applicable
                         Planned - Requires POAM

_____

_____

_____

_____

3.1.18 Control connection of mobile devices.

☐ Implemented   ☐ Not Implemented -   ☐ Not Applicable
                         Planned - Requires POAM

_____

_____

3.1.19 Encrypt CUI on mobile devices and mobile computing platforms.

☐ Implemented   ☐ Not Implemented -   ☐ Not Applicable
                           Planned - Requires POAM

3.1.20 Verify and control/limit connections to and use of external systems.

☐ Implemented   ☐ Not Implemented -   ☐ Not Applicable
                           Planned - Requires POAM

3.1.21 Limit use of organizational portable storage devices on external systems.

☐ Implemented   ☐ Not Implemented -   ☐ Not Applicable
                           Planned - Requires POAM

_____

_____

3.1.22 Control CUI posted or processed on publicly accessible systems.

☐ Implemented   ☐ Not Implemented -   ☐ Not Applicable
                           Planned - Requires POAM

_____

_____

_____

_____

_____

Awareness and Training (AT)

Awareness and Training is about an active cybersecurity training program for employees and a recurring education program that ensures their familiarity and compliance with protecting sensitive and CUI/CDI company data consistently. The websites (below) identify FREE government-sponsored sites a company can leverage without expending any of its own resources. The three major training requirements that can be expected of most vendors supporting federal government contract activities include:

1. **Cybersecurity Awareness Training.**
   https://securityawareness.usalearning.gov/cybersecurity/index.htm

2. **Insider Threat Training.**
   https://securityawareness.usalearning.gov/itawareness/index.htm
   (More discussion on the "Insider Threat" topic See Control 3.2.3).

3. **Privacy.**
   https://iatraining.disa.mil/eta/piiv2/launchPage.htm (This would specifically apply to any company that handles, processes or maintains Personally Identifiable Information (PII) and Personal Health Information (PHI). The author's expectation is that even though a company does not handle PII or PHI, the federal government to make this a universal training requirement.)

3.2.1 Ensure that managers, systems administrators, and users of organizational systems are made aware of the security risks associated with their activities and of the applicable policies, standards, and procedures related to the security of those systems.

☐ Implemented   ☐ Not Implemented - Planned - Requires POAM   ☐ Not Applicable

_____

_____

_____

_____

3.2.2 Ensure that organizational personnel are adequately trained to carry out their assigned information security-related duties and responsibilities.

☐ Implemented   ☐ Not Implemented -   ☐ Not Applicable
                            Planned - Requires POAM

_____

_____

_____

_____

3.2.3 Provide security awareness training on recognizing and reporting potential indicators of insider threat.

☐ Implemented   ☐ Not Implemented -   ☐ Not Applicable
                            Planned - Requires POAM

_____

_____

_____

_____

_____

Audit and Accountability (AU)

The AU control is primarily about the ability of the system owner/company to monitor unauthorized access to the system through system logging functions of the Operating System and other network devices such as firewalls. A SA is typically assigned the duty to review log files; these may include both authorized and unauthorized access to the network, applications, databases, financial systems, etc. Most businesses will rely on manual review; however, some "smart" servers and firewalls can provide automated alerts to IT personnel of unauthorized use or intrusion. The key is to understand the auditing capabilities of the corporate system and be prepared to defend its capabilities and limitations if government representatives or third-party assessors request proof of control compliance.

```
...sion Detection System

.**]  [1:1407:9] SNMP trap udp [**]
[Classification: Attempted Information Leak] [Priority: 2]
03/06-8:14:09.082119 192.168.1.167:1052 -> 172.30.128.27:162
UDP TTL:118 TOS:0x0 ID:29101 IpLen:20 DgmLen:87

Personal Firewall

3/6/2006 8:14:07 AM, "Rule ""Block Windows File Sharing"" blocked (192.168.1.54,
netbios-ssn(139)).", "Rule ""Block Windows File Sharing"" blocked (192.168.1.54,
netbios-ssn(139)).  Inbound TCP connection.  Local address,service is
(KENT(172.30.128.27),netbios-ssn(139)).  Remote address,service is
(192.168.1.54,39923).  Process name is ""System"".""

3/3/2006 9:04:04 AM, Firewall configuration updated: 398 rules., Firewall configuration
updated: 398 rules.

Antivirus Software, Log 1

3/4/2006 9:33:50 AM, Definition File Download, KENT, userk, Definition downloader
3/4/2006 9:33:09 AM, AntiVirus Startup, KENT, userk, System
3/3/2006 3:56:46 PM, AntiVirus Shutdown, KENT, userk, System

Antivirus Software, Log 2

240203071234,16,3,7,KENT,userk,,,,,,16777216,"Virus definitions are
current.",0,,0,,,,,0,,,,,,,,,SAVPROD,{ xxxxxxxxx-xxxx-xxxx-xxxx-xxxxxxxxxxxx },End
User,(IP)-192.168.1.121.,GROUP,0:0:0:0:0:0,9.0.0.338,,,,,,,,,,,,,,

Antispyware Software

DSO Exploit: Data source object exploit (Registry change, nothing done) HKEY_USERS\S-
1-5-19\Software\Microsoft\Windows\CurrentVersion\Internet Settings\Zones\0\1004!=W=?
```

Audit log type examples. The logs above are good examples of the system logs that should be reviewed regularly. These are the business's responsibility to monitor the network actively. Another term of high interest is **Continuous Monitoring (ConMon).** ConMon can be accomplished by both manual and automated means, and auditing is a major control family supporting the objectives of this cybersecurity principle.

3.3.1 Create and retain system audit logs and records to the extent needed to enable the monitoring, analysis, investigation, and reporting of unlawful or unauthorized system activity.

☐ Implemented   ☐ Not Implemented -   ☐ Not Applicable
                         Planned - Requires POAM

_____

_____

_____

3.3.2 Ensure that the actions of individual system users can be uniquely traced to those users, so they can be held accountable for their actions.

☐ Implemented   ☐ Not Implemented -   ☐ Not Applicable
                         Planned - Requires POAM

_____

_____

_____

_____

_____

3.3.3 Review and update logged events.

☐ Implemented   ☐ Not Implemented -   ☐ Not Applicable
                         Planned - Requires POAM

_____

_____

_____

_____

3.3.4 Alert in the event of an audit logging process failure.

☐ Implemented   ☐ Not Implemented -   ☐ Not Applicable
                          Planned - Requires POAM

_____

_____

_____

_____

3.3.5 Correlate audit record review, analysis, and reporting processes for investigation and response to indications of unlawful, unauthorized, suspicious, or unusual activity.

☐ Implemented   ☐ Not Implemented -   ☐ Not Applicable
                          Planned - Requires POAM

_____

_____

_____

_____

3.3.6 Provide audit record reduction and report generation to support on-demand analysis and reporting.

☐ Implemented   ☐ Not Implemented -   ☐ Not Applicable
                          Planned - Requires POAM

_____

_____

3.3.7 Provide a system capability that compares and synchronizes internal system clocks with an authoritative source to generate time stamps for audit records.

☐ Implemented   ☐ Not Implemented -   ☐ Not Applicable
Planned - Requires POAM

3.3.8 Protect audit information and audit logging tools from unauthorized access, modification, and deletion.

☐ Implemented   ☐ Not Implemented -   ☐ Not Applicable
Planned - Requires POAM

3.3.9 Limit management of audit logging functionality to a subset of privileged users.

☐ Implemented   ☐ Not Implemented - Planned - Requires POAM   ☐ Not Applicable

_____

_____

_____

_____

_____

Configuration Management (CM)

The real importance of Configuration Management is it is, in fact, the "opposite side of the same coin" called cybersecurity. CM is used to track and confirm changes to the system's baseline; this could be changed in hardware, firmware, and software that would alert IT professionals to unauthorized changes to the IT environment. CM is used to confirm and ensure programmatic controls prevent changes that have not been adequately tested or approved.

CM requires establishing baselines for tracking, controlling, and managing a business's internal IT infrastructure specific to NIST 800-171. Companies with an effective CM process need to consider information security implications for the development and operation of information systems. This will include the active management of changes to company hardware, software, and documentation.

Effective CM of information systems requires the integration of the management of secure configurations into the CM process. If good CM exists as a well-defined "change" process, protection of the IT environment is more assured. This should be considered as the second most important security control. It is suggested that both management and IT personnel have adequate knowledge and training to maintain this process since it is so integral to good programmatic and cyber security practice.

3.4.1 Establish and maintain baseline configurations and inventories of organizational systems (including hardware, software, firmware, and documentation) throughout the respective system development life cycles.

☐ Implemented   ☐ Not Implemented -   ☐ Not Applicable
                              Planned - Requires POAM

_____

_____

_____

_____

3.4.2 Establish and enforce security configuration settings for information technology products employed in organizational systems.

☐ Implemented   ☐ Not Implemented -   ☐ Not Applicable
                         Planned - Requires POAM

_____

_____

_____

_____

3.4.3 Track, review, approve or disapprove, and log changes to organizational systems.

☐ Implemented   ☐ Not Implemented -   ☐ Not Applicable
                         Planned - Requires POAM

_____

_____

_____

_____

3.4.4 Analyze the security impact of changes prior to implementation.

☐ Implemented   ☐ Not Implemented -   ☐ Not Applicable
                         Planned - Requires POAM

_____

_____

_____

3.4.5 Define, document, approve, and enforce physical and logical access restrictions associated with changes to organizational systems.

☐ Implemented   ☐ Not Implemented -   ☐ Not Applicable
                              Planned - Requires POAM

_____

_____

_____

_____

3.4.6 Employ the principle of least functionality by configuring organizational systems to provide only essential capabilities.

☐ Implemented   ☐ Not Implemented -   ☐ Not Applicable
                              Planned - Requires POAM

_____

_____

_____

_____

3.4.7 Restrict, disable, or prevent the use of nonessential programs, functions, ports, protocols, and services.

☐ Implemented   ☐ Not Implemented -   ☐ Not Applicable
                              Planned - Requires POAM

_____

_____

_____

_____

3.4.8 Apply deny-by-exception (blacklisting) policy to prevent the use of unauthorized software or deny-all, permit-by-exception (whitelisting) policy to allow the execution of authorized software.

☐ Implemented   ☐ Not Implemented -   ☐ Not Applicable
                          Planned - Requires POAM

_____

_____

_____

_____

3.4.9 Control and monitor user-installed software.

☐ Implemented   ☐ Not Implemented -   ☐ Not Applicable
                          Planned - Requires POAM

_____

_____

_____

_____

_____

Identification and Authentication (IA)

The 2015 Office of Personnel Management (OPM) breach could have been prevented if this control family was properly implemented and enforced. The one "positive" effect that the OPM breach caused for federal agencies was the requirement from Congress that these requirements became mandatory. Congress's focus on the use of Two-Factor Authentication (2FA) and Multi-Factor Authentication (MFA) has provided constructive results for the federal government and impetus for more stringent cybersecurity measures beyond the government's IT boundaries.

While some businesses will be afforded, for example, Common Access Cards (CAC) or Personal Identity Verification (PIV) cards to accomplish 2FA between the company and the government, most won't be authorized such access. Implementation will require various levels of investment, and the use of 2FA devices, or also called "tokens." This too will require additional financial costs and technical integration challenges for the average business.

For many small businesses, this will also require some sizeable investments on the part of the company and a clear commitment to working with the government. Solutions could include, for example, RSA® tokens—these are small devices that constantly rotate a security variable (a key) that a user enters in addition to a password or Personal Identification Number (PIN). This solution affords one potential solution to businesses to meet the 2FA requirement.

According to The House Committee on Oversight and Government Reform report on September 7th, 2016, OPM's leadership failed to "implement basic cyber hygiene, such as maintaining current authorities to operate and employing strong multi-factor authentication, despite years of warning from the Inspector General... tools were available that could have prevented the breaches..." (SOURCE: https://oversight.house.gov/wp-content/uploads/2016/09/The-OPM-Data-Breach-How-the-Government-Jeopardized-Our-National-Security-for-More-than-a-Generation.pdf*)*

The best approaches will require good market surveys of the available resources and be mindful that two-factor does not need to be a card or token solution. Other options would include biometrics (fingerprints, facial recognition, etc.) or Short Message Service (SMS) 2FA solution as used by Amazon® to verify its customers. They use a Two-Step verification process that provides a "verification code sent to the customer's personal cell phone or home phone to verify their identity.

Be prepared to do serious "homework" on these controls, and research all potential solutions. Once this control is resolved, the company will be in a better position not just with the government but have serious answers that will ensure the protection of its sensitive data.

3.5.1 Identify system users, processes acting on behalf of users, and devices.

☐ Implemented   ☐ Not Implemented -   ☐ Not Applicable
                                Planned - Requires POAM

_____

_____

_____

_____

3.5.2 Authenticate (or verify) the identities of users, processes, or devices, as a prerequisite to allowing access to organizational systems.

☐ Implemented   ☐ Not Implemented -   ☐ Not Applicable
                                Planned - Requires POAM

_____

_____

_____

_____

3.5.3 Use multifactor authentication for local and network access to privileged accounts and for network access to non-privileged accounts.

☐ Implemented   ☐ Not Implemented -   ☐ Not Applicable
                                Planned - Requires POAM

_____

_____

_____

_____

3.5.4 **Employ replay-resistant authentication mechanisms for network access to privileged and non-privileged accounts.**

☐ Implemented   ☐ Not Implemented -   ☐ Not Applicable
                          Planned - Requires POAM

_____

_____

_____

_____

_____

3.5.5 **Prevent reuse of identifiers for a defined period.**

☐ Implemented   ☐ Not Implemented -   ☐ Not Applicable
                          Planned - Requires POAM

_____

_____

_____

_____

3.5.6 **Disable identifiers after a defined period of inactivity.**

☐ Implemented   ☐ Not Implemented -   ☐ Not Applicable
                          Planned - Requires POAM

_____

_____

3.5.7 Enforce a minimum password complexity and change of characters when new passwords are created.

☐ Implemented ☐ Not Implemented - ☐ Not Applicable
Planned - Requires POAM

3.5.8 Prohibit password reuse for a specified number of generations.

☐ Implemented ☐ Not Implemented - ☐ Not Applicable
Planned - Requires POAM

3.5.9 Allow temporary password use for system logons with an immediate change to a permanent password.

☐ Implemented ☐ Not Implemented - ☐ Not Applicable
Planned - Requires POAM

_____

_____

3.5.10 Store and transmit only cryptographically-protected passwords.

☐ Implemented   ☐ Not Implemented -   ☐ Not Applicable
                                               Planned - Requires POAM

_____

_____

_____

_____

3.5.11 Obscure feedback of authentication information.

☐ Implemented   ☐ Not Implemented -   ☐ Not Applicable
                                               Planned - Requires POAM

_____

_____

_____

_____

_____

Incident Response (IR)

Incident Response (IR) primarily requires a plan, an identification of who or what agency is notified when a breach has occurred and testing of the plan over time. This control requires the development of an Incident Response Plan (IRP). There are many templates available online, and if there is an existing relationship with a federal agency, companies should be able to obtain agency-specific templates.

OCCURRENCE →EVENT → INCIDENT
(less defined/initial occurrence) → (defined/confirmed/high impact)
Incident Response Spectrum

The first effort should be identifying with government representatives what constitutes a reportable event that formally becomes an incident. This could include a confirmed breach that has occurred to the IT infrastructure. Incidents could include anything from a Denial of Service (DOS) attack—an overloading of outwardly facing web or mail servers--, or exfiltration of data—where CUI/CDI and corporate data has been copied or moved to outside of the company's firewall/perimeter. Incidents could also include the destruction of data that the company's IT staff, for example, identifies through ongoing audit activities.

Secondarily, who do you notify? Do you alert your assigned Contract Officer Representative (COR), the Contract Office, DOD's US Cybercommand at Fort Meade, MD, or possibly the Department of Homeland Security's (DHS) Computer Emergency Response Team (CERT) (https://www.us-cert.gov/forms/report)? Company representatives will have to ask their assigned COR where to file standard government "incident" reports. They should be able to provide templates and forms specific to the agency.

Finally, this security control will require testing at least *annually*, but more often is recommended. Until comfortable with the IR "reporting chain," ***practice, practice, practice***.

3.6.1 Establish an operational incident-handling capability for organizational systems that includes preparation, detection, analysis, containment, recovery, and user response activities.

☐ Implemented   ☐ Not Implemented -   ☐ Not Applicable
                      Planned - Requires POAM

3.6.2 Track, document, and report incidents to designated officials and/or authorities both internal and external to the organization.

☐ Implemented   ☐ Not Implemented -   ☐ Not Applicable
                                              Planned - Requires POAM

_____

_____

_____

_____

3.6.3 Test the organizational incident response capability

☐ Implemented   ☐ Not Implemented -   ☐ Not Applicable
                                              Planned - Requires POAM

_____

_____

_____

_____

Maintenance (MA)

The MA security control is relatively easy to address with regards to the requirements of NIST 800-171. This control requires processes and procedures that provide oversight of third-party vendors that offer IT maintenance and support. While this may appear vaguely paranoid, the company is required to exercise control of all maintenance personnel that potentially will have access to the company's and government's resident CUI/CDI and data. This will also typically require company escorts whose background have been properly checked and authorized to oversee outside workers.

Lack of maintenance or a failure to perform maintenance can result in the unauthorized disclosure of CUI/CDI. The full implementation of this requirement is contingent on the finalization of the proposed CUI/CDI federal regulation and marking guidance in the **CUI Registry**. (The marking requirements have been completed, and it is best to refer to the Registry, https://www.archives.gov/cui/registry/category-list, for specified industry codes.) These markings should be applied to business CUI/CDI data as well as IT hardware such as servers, desktops, laptops, etc.

3.7.1 Perform maintenance on organizational systems.

☐ Implemented   ☐ Not Implemented -   ☐ Not Applicable
                          Planned - Requires POAM

_____

_____

_____

_____

3.7.2 Provide controls on the tools, techniques, mechanisms, and personnel used to conduct system maintenance.

☐ Implemented   ☐ Not Implemented -   ☐ Not Applicable
                          Planned - Requires POAM

_____

_____

3.7.3 Ensure equipment removed for off-site maintenance is sanitized of any CUI.

☐ Implemented   ☐ Not Implemented -   ☐ Not Applicable
                                  Planned - Requires POAM

_____

_____

_____

_____

3.7.4 Check media containing diagnostic and test programs for malicious code before the media are used in organizational systems.

☐ Implemented   ☐ Not Implemented -   ☐ Not Applicable
                                  Planned - Requires POAM

_____

_____

_____

_____

3.7.5 Require multifactor authentication to establish nonlocal maintenance sessions via external network connections and terminate such connections when nonlocal maintenance is complete.

☐ Implemented   ☐ Not Implemented -   ☐ Not Applicable
                                Planned - Requires POAM

_____

_____

_____

_____

3.7.6 Supervise the maintenance activities of maintenance personnel without required access authorization.

☐ Implemented   ☐ Not Implemented -   ☐ Not Applicable
                                Planned - Requires POAM

_____

_____

_____

_____

_____

Media Protection (MP)

The MP control was written to handle the challenges of managing and protecting the computer media storing CUI/CDI. This would include the governments' concerns about removable hard drives and especially the ability for a threat employ the use of a Universal Serial Bus (USB) "thumb drive."

While most computer users are aware of the convenience of the thumb drive to help store, transfer, and maintain data, it is also a well-known threat vector where criminals and foreign threats can introduce serious malware and viruses into unsuspecting users' computers; the DOD forbids their use except under very specific and controlled instances.

MP is also about assurances by the business that proper destruction and sanitization of old storage devices has occurred. There are many instances where federal agencies have not implemented an effective sanitization process, and inadvertent disclosure of national security data has been released to the public. Cases include salvage companies discovering hard drives and disposed computers containing CUI/CDI and, in several cases, national security classified information, has occurred.

Be especially mindful that the sanitization process requires high-grade industry or government-approved applications that completely and effectively destroys all data on the target drive. Other processes may include physical shredding of the drive or destruction methods that further prevent the reconstruction of any virtual data by unauthorized personnel.

3.8.1 Protect (i.e., physically control and securely store) system media containing CUI, both paper and digital.

☐ Implemented   ☐ Not Implemented -   ☐ Not Applicable
                          Planned - Requires POAM

3.8.2 Limit access to CUI on system media to authorized users.

☐ Implemented   ☐ Not Implemented -   ☐ Not Applicable
                            Planned - Requires POAM

_____

_____

_____

_____

3.8.3 Sanitize or destroy system media containing CUI before disposal or release for reuse.

☐ Implemented   ☐ Not Implemented -   ☐ Not Applicable
                            Planned - Requires POAM

_____

_____

_____

_____

3.8.4 Mark media with necessary CUI markings and distribution limitations.

☐ Implemented   ☐ Not Implemented -   ☐ Not Applicable
                            Planned - Requires POAM

_____

_____

_____

_____

3.8.5 Control access to media containing CUI and maintain accountability for media during transport outside of controlled areas.

☐ Implemented ☐ Not Implemented - Planned - Requires POAM ☐ Not Applicable

_____

_____

_____

_____

3.8.6 Implement cryptographic mechanisms to protect the confidentiality of CUI stored on digital media during transport unless otherwise protected by alternative physical safeguards.

☐ Implemented ☐ Not Implemented - Planned - Requires POAM ☐ Not Applicable

_____

_____

_____

_____

3.8.7 Control the use of removable media on system components.

☐ Implemented ☐ Not Implemented - Planned - Requires POAM ☐ Not Applicable

_____

_____

_____

_____

_____

3.8.8 **Prohibit the use of portable storage devices when such devices have no identifiable owner.**

☐ Implemented   ☐ Not Implemented -   ☐ Not Applicable
                        Planned - Requires POAM

_____

_____

_____

_____

3.8.9 **Protect the confidentiality of backup CUI at storage locations.**

☐ Implemented   ☐ Not Implemented -   ☐ Not Applicable
                        Planned - Requires POAM

_____

_____

_____

_____

_____

Personnel Security (PS)

This is a relatively simple control. It most likely is already implemented within the company and only requires procedural documents are provided in the submission. This should include both civil and criminal background checks using a reputable company that can process the individual background checks through the Federal Bureau of Investigation (FBI). Background Checking companies can also do other forms of personnel checks to include individual social media presence or financial solvency matters that may avoid any future embarrassment for the company.

While these checks are not well defined for company's under NIST 800-171, it should meet minimum government standards for a **Public Trust** review. Discuss with the Contract Officer what the requirements they suggest be met to provide the level of background check required to meet the NIST 800-171 requirement. Also, it is always best to work with HR and legal experts when formulating a personnel security policy to include the types and kinds of investigations are in accordance with applicable state and federal law in this area.

3.9.1 Screen individuals prior to authorizing access to organizational systems containing CUI.

☐ Implemented   ☐ Not Implemented -   ☐ Not Applicable
                         Planned - Requires POAM

_____

_____

_____

_____

3.9.2 Ensure that organizational systems containing CUI are protected during and after personnel actions such as terminations and transfers.

☐ Implemented   ☐ Not Implemented -   ☐ Not Applicable
                         Planned - Requires POAM

_____

_____

Physical Protection (PP)

Physical security is part of a company's overall protection of its people and facilities. A little-known fact is that the guiding principle for any *true* cybersecurity professional is to protect the life and safety of the people supported. This control is also about the protection of damage to corporate assets, facilities, or equipment; this includes any loss or destruction of the material computer equipment secured by the PP security control. This controls addresses the physical security that also includes such elements as guards, alarm systems, cameras, etc., that help the company protect its sensitive company data and, of course, its NIST 800-171 CUI.

There are no limits on how to harden a company's "castle walls," but for any owner, the cost is always a major consideration. Protecting vital CUI/CDI while seemingly expansive under this control allows for reasonable flexibility. Again, the company should reasonably define its success under the NIST 800-171 controls. "Success" can be defined from the company's point of view regarding complexity or cost but must be prepared to defend any proposed solution to government assessors.

3.10.1 Limit physical access to organizational systems, equipment, and the respective operating environments to authorized individuals.

☐ Implemented   ☐ Not Implemented -   ☐ Not Applicable
                          Planned - Requires POAM

_____

_____

_____

_____

3.10.2 Protect and monitor the physical facility and support infrastructure for organizational systems.

☐ Implemented   ☐ Not Implemented -   ☐ Not Applicable
                          Planned - Requires POAM

_____

_____

_____

_____

3.10.3 Escort visitors and monitor visitor activity.

☐ Implemented   ☐ Not Implemented -   ☐ Not Applicable
                        Planned - Requires POAM

_____

_____

_____

_____

3.10.4 Maintain audit logs of physical access.

☐ Implemented   ☐ Not Implemented -   ☐ Not Applicable
                        Planned - Requires POAM

_____

_____

_____

_____

3.10.5 Control and manage physical access devices.

☐ Implemented   ☐ Not Implemented -   ☐ Not Applicable
                        Planned - Requires POAM

_____

_____

_____

_____

3.10.6 Enforce safeguarding measures for CUI at alternate work sites.

☐ Implemented   ☐ Not Implemented -   ☐ Not Applicable
                         Planned - Requires POAM

_____

_____

_____

_____

_____

Risk Assessment (RA)

The RA control relies on a continual process to determine whether changes in hardware, software or architecture create either a major positive or negative **security-relevant** effect. This is typically done by using a **Change Request** (CR). If an upgrade to, for example, the Window 10 ® Secure Host Baseline Operating System software, and it improves the security posture of the network, a Risk Assessment (RA) is needed and associated **risk analysis** should be performed by authorized technical personnel. This could take the form of a technical report that management accepts from its IT staff for approval or disapproval of the change. Management, working with its IT staff, should determine thresholds when a formal RA activity needs to occur.

The RA process affords a great amount of flexibility during the life of the system and should be used when other-than, for example, a new application or **security patches** are applied. Security patches updates are typically integrated into Operating Systems and applications. IT personnel should also regularly manually check for normal functional patches and security patch updates from the software companies' websites.

"Negative" security-relevant effects on the corporate IT infrastructure include, for example, a major re-architecture event or a move to a Cloud Service Provider. While these events may not seem "negative," NIST standards require a full reassessment. In other words, plan accordingly if the company is going to embark on a major overhaul of its IT system. There will be a need under these circumstances to consider the impacts to the company's current Authority to Operate (ATO). These types of event typically necessitate that the NIST 800-171 process is redone; prior work in terms of policies and procedures can be reused to receive an updated ATO.

3.11.1 Periodically assess the risk to organizational operations (including mission, functions, image, or reputation), organizational assets, and individuals, resulting from the operation of organizational systems and the associated processing, storage, or transmission of CUI.

☐ Implemented   ☐ Not Implemented -   ☐ Not Applicable
                         Planned - Requires POAM

3.11.2 Scan for vulnerabilities in organizational systems and applications periodically and when new vulnerabilities affecting those systems and applications are identified.

☐ Implemented ☐ Not Implemented - ☐ Not Applicable
Planned - Requires POAM

_____

_____

_____

_____

3.11.3 Remediate vulnerabilities in accordance with risk assessments.

☐ Implemented ☐ Not Implemented - ☐ Not Applicable
Planned - Requires POAM

_____

_____

_____

_____

Security Assessment (SA)

The SA control is about a process that re-assesses the state of all security controls and whether changes have occurred requiring additional mitigations of new risks or threats. The standard is 1/3rd of the controls are to be re-assessed annually. This would require designated IT personnel conduct a SA event of approximately 36-37 controls per year. This should be captured in what is called a **ConMon Plan**.

Continuous Monitoring is a key component of the NIST 800 series cybersecurity protection framework. It is defined as "...maintaining ongoing awareness of information security, vulnerabilities, and threats to support organizational risk management decisions," (NIST Special Publication 800-137, *Information Security Continuous Monitoring (ISCM) for Federal Information Systems and Organizations*, http://nvlpubs.nist.gov/nistpubs/Legacy/SP/nistspecialpublication800-137.pdf).

3.12.1 Periodically assess the security controls in organizational systems to determine if the controls are effective in their application.

☐ Implemented   ☐ Not Implemented -   ☐ Not Applicable
                              Planned - Requires POAM

3.12.2 Develop and implement plans of action designed to correct deficiencies and reduce or eliminate vulnerabilities in organizational systems.

☐ Implemented   ☐ Not Implemented -   ☐ Not Applicable
                              Planned - Requires POAM

_____

_____

3.12.3 **Monitor security controls on an ongoing basis to ensure the continued effectiveness of the controls.**

☐ Implemented   ☐ Not Implemented -   ☐ Not Applicable
                          Planned - Requires POAM

_____

_____

_____

_____

3.12.4 **Develop, document, and periodically update system security plans that describe system boundaries, system environments of operation, how security requirements are implemented, and the relationships with or connections to other systems.**

☐ Implemented   ☐ Not Implemented -   ☐ Not Applicable
                          Planned - Requires POAM

_____

_____

_____

_____

_____

System and Communications Protection (SC)

The overall risk management strategy is a key in establishing the appropriate technical solutions as well as procedural direction and guidance for the company. The core of this security control is it establishes policy based upon applicable federal laws, Executive Orders, directives, regulations, policies, standards, and guidance. This control focuses on information security policy that can reflect the complexity of a business and its operation with the government. The procedures should be established for the security of the overall IT architecture and specifically for the components (hardware and software) of the information system.

In this control, many of the prior reinforcing controls can be used in demonstrating to the government a fuller understanding of NIST 800-171 requirements. The apparent repetition of other already developed technical solutions and procedural guides can be used as supporting these controls. However, it is important that corporate procedures are addressed individually—this is for traceability purposes of any potential current or future audit of the company's work by the government; clear and aligned explanations of the controls will make the approval process quicker.

3.13.1 Monitor, control, and protect communications (i.e., information transmitted or received by organizational systems) at the external boundaries and key internal boundaries of organizational systems.

☐ Implemented   ☐ Not Implemented -   ☐ Not Applicable
                          Planned - Requires POAM

3.13.2 Employ architectural designs, software development techniques, and systems engineering principles that promote effective information security within organizational systems.

☐ Implemented   ☐ Not Implemented -   ☐ Not Applicable
                              Planned - Requires POAM

_____

_____

_____

_____

3.13.3 Separate user functionality from system management functionality.

☐ Implemented   ☐ Not Implemented -   ☐ Not Applicable
                              Planned - Requires POAM

_____

_____

_____

_____

3.13.4 Prevent unauthorized and unintended information transfer via shared system resources.

☐ Implemented   ☐ Not Implemented -   ☐ Not Applicable
                              Planned - Requires POAM

_____

_____

_____

_____

3.13.5 Implement subnetworks for publicly accessible system components that are physically or logically separated from internal networks.

☐ Implemented ☐ Not Implemented - Planned - Requires POAM ☐ Not Applicable

_____

_____

_____

_____

3.13.6 Deny network communications traffic by default and allow network communications traffic by exception (i.e., deny all, permit by exception).

☐ Implemented ☐ Not Implemented - Planned - Requires POAM ☐ Not Applicable

_____

_____

_____

_____

3.13.7 Prevent remote devices from simultaneously establishing non-remote connections with organizational systems and communicating via some other connection to resources in external networks (i.e., split tunneling).

☐ Implemented ☐ Not Implemented - Planned - Requires POAM ☐ Not Applicable

_____

_____

3.13.8 Implement cryptographic mechanisms to prevent unauthorized disclosure of CUI during transmission unless otherwise protected by alternative physical safeguards.

☐ Implemented   ☐ Not Implemented -   ☐ Not Applicable
                                  Planned - Requires POAM

3.13.9 Terminate network connections associated with communications sessions at the end of the sessions or after a defined period of inactivity.

☐ Implemented   ☐ Not Implemented -   ☐ Not Applicable
                                  Planned - Requires POAM

3.13.10 Establish and manage cryptographic keys for cryptography employed in organizational systems.

☐ Implemented   ☐ Not Implemented -   ☐ Not Applicable
                                  Planned - Requires POAM

3.13.11 Employ FIPS-validated cryptography when used to protect the confidentiality of CUI.

☐ Implemented   ☐ Not Implemented -   ☐ Not Applicable
                    Planned - Requires POAM

3.13.12 Prohibit remote activation of collaborative computing devices and provide indication of devices in use to users present at the device.

☐ Implemented   ☐ Not Implemented -   ☐ Not Applicable
                    Planned - Requires POAM

3.13.13 Control and monitor the use of mobile code.

☐ Implemented   ☐ Not Implemented -   ☐ Not Applicable
                    Planned - Requires POAM

3.13.14 Control and monitor the use of Voice over Internet Protocol (VoIP) technologies.

☐ Implemented   ☐ Not Implemented -   ☐ Not Applicable
Planned - Requires POAM

3.13.15 Protect the authenticity of communications sessions.

☐ Implemented   ☐ Not Implemented -   ☐ Not Applicable
Planned - Requires POAM

3.13.16 Protect the confidentiality of CUI at rest.

☐ Implemented   ☐ Not Implemented -   ☐ Not Applicable
Planned - Requires POAM

System and Information Integrity (SI)

This control family is about maintaining the integrity of data within the company's system security boundary. It primarily defended by active measures such as anti-virus and malware protection. This control addresses the establishment of procedures for effective implementation of the security controls. Cybersecurity policies and procedures may include Information Security (INFOSEC) policies. Company risk management strategy is a key factor in establishing decisive system protections.

3.14.1 Identify, report, and correct system flaws in a timely manner.

☐ Implemented   ☐ Not Implemented -   ☐ Not Applicable
                          Planned - Requires POAM

_____

_____

_____

_____

3.14.2 Provide protection from malicious code at designated locations within organizational systems.

☐ Implemented   ☐ Not Implemented -   ☐ Not Applicable
                          Planned - Requires POAM

_____

_____

_____

_____

3.14.3 Monitor system security alerts and advisories and take action in response.

☐ Implemented   ☐ Not Implemented -   ☐ Not Applicable
                                Planned - Requires POAM

_____

_____

_____

_____

3.14.4 Update malicious code protection mechanisms when new releases are available.

☐ Implemented   ☐ Not Implemented -   ☐ Not Applicable
                                Planned - Requires POAM

_____

_____

_____

_____

3.14.5 Perform periodic scans of organizational systems and real-time scans of files from external sources as files are downloaded, opened, or executed.

☐ Implemented   ☐ Not Implemented -   ☐ Not Applicable
                                Planned - Requires POAM

_____

_____

_____

_____

3.14.6 Monitor organizational systems, including inbound and outbound communications traffic, to detect attacks and indicators of potential attacks.

☐ Implemented   ☐ Not Implemented -   ☐ Not Applicable
                          Planned - Requires POAM

_____

_____

_____

_____

3.14.7 Identify unauthorized use of organizational systems.

☐ Implemented   ☐ Not Implemented -   ☐ Not Applicable
                          Planned - Requires POAM

_____

_____

_____

_____

ANNEX A – Hardware List Example

<IS System Name Here> Approved Hardware

System item	Subsys	Manufacturer	Item	Serial No.	Model	Type/Function	Source (Vendor, Reseller, etc.)	IA Enabled (Yes/No)
					Computers			
		HP	Laptop		8460	Laptop	HP	No
		HP	Laptop		8470	Laptop	HP	No
		HP	Laptop		8570	Laptop	HP	No
		HP	Desktop		DC8200	Desktop	HP	No
		EpicData	Terminal/Time Clock		Umvmsr-02	Terminal/Time Clock	EpicData	No
		TekPanel	Shared Device		550T	VMS	TekPanel	No
		TekPanel	Shared Device		460T	VMS	TekPanel	No
		TekPanel	Shared Device		420T	VMS	TekPanel	No
		Dell	Tablet		Venue 11 Pro (7130/7139/7310-	Tablet	Dell	No
		Panasonic	Tablet		ToughPad FZ-G1	Tablet	Panasonic	
					NAS/SAN			
		EMC	NAS		VNX5700	NAS	HP	No
		HP	Tape Library		ESL_G3	Tape Library	HP	No
		Brocade	Fibre Switch		DS300B	NAS Fibre Switch	EMC	No
		Overland	Tape Library		NEO 8000E	Tape library	HP	No
					Printers/Scanners			
		HP	Plotter		T1100PS	Network Plotter	HP	No
		HP	Plotter		T1120PS	Network Plotter	HP	No
		HP	Plotter		DJ1200	Network Plotter	HP	No
		HP	Plotter		T1300PS	Network Plotter	HP	No
		HP	Printer		CP5535DN	Network Printer	HP	No
		HP	Printer		CP5550	Network Printer	HP	No
		HP	Printer		CP4025	Network Printer	HP	No
		HP	Printer		LaserJet Pro 400	Personal Printer	HP	No
		Primera	CD Printer		Bravo II	CD Printer	Primera	No
		Pryor	Engraver		Maktronic 3000 BenchDot Stylus R2000	Engraver	Pryor	No
		Epson	Printer			Personal Printer	Epson	No
		Fujitsu	Scanner		ScanSnap ix500	Scanner	FUJITSU	No
		Fujitsu	Scanner		Scanmap S1500	Scanner	FUJITSU	No
					Servers			
		HP	Server		DL585-G7	Server	HP	No
		HP	Server		DL585-G8	Server	HP	No
		SCN	Server		M3000	Server	SCN	No
		McAfee	Server		MVM3100	Vulnerability Scanner	McAfee	No
		Foundstone	Server		FS1000	Server	Foundstone	No
					Network			
		Cisco	Switch		4506	Switch	Cisco	Yes
		Cisco	Switch		3750	Switch	Cisco	Yes
		Juniper	Firewall		SSG-140-SH	LKE VPN Router	Juniper	Yes
		Infoblox	DNS/DHCP		820	DNS/DHCP Appliance	Infoblox	Yes

(This fillable template is currently available at:
https://cybersentinel.tech/product/template-premium-hardware-list/)

**CONTROLLED UNCLASSIFIED INFORMATION (CUI)/
CRITICAL DEFENSE INFORMATION (CDI)
[when filled in for ALL pages]**

\<IS System Name Here\> Approved Software [Please remove software here not used]

'C' for Commercial Off-The-Shelf
'S' for Open Source
'G' for Government Off-The-Shelf
'F' for freeware.

Vendor	SW Purpose	Retailer	SW Type	is IA or IA Enabled	Country of Origin	NIAP Evaluated
McAfee		McAfee	C	Yes		
PTC	Graphics tool - Publications	PTC	C	No		
Microsoft Corporation	Part of Visual Studio Professional Pro Ver.:	Microsoft Corporation	C	No		
AT&T	Internet connecter	AT&T	G	No		
AMD Catalyst	Graphics control	AMD w/hardware	C	No		
A.utodesk, Inc	3d digital designer	Autodesk, Inc	C	No		
Autodesk, Inc	Part of AutoCAD 2011 - English	Autodesk, Inc	C	No		
Autolt Team	automation language	Autolt Team	F	No		
Avecto		Avecto	C	No		
DoD	Classification Banner Display	DoD	G	Yes		
Microsoft Corporation		Microsoft Corporation	C	No		
Jerico Inc.	Data Erasure	Jerico Inc.	C	No		
Scooter Software	File/Folder Mgmt	Scooter Software	C	No		
Biscom	Fax	Biscom	"	No		
.... .	.	"		:		

(This fillable template currently available at: https://cybersentinel.tech/product/template-premium-software-listing/)

ANNEX C – Relevant References

Federal Information Security Modernization Act of 2014 (P.L. 113-283), December 2014.
http://www.gpo.gov/fdsys/pkg/PLAW-113publ283/pdf/PLAW-113publ283.pdf

Executive Order 13556, *Controlled Unclassified Information*, November 2010.
http://www.gpo.gov/fdsys/pkg/FR-2010-11-09/pdf/2010-28360.pdf

Executive Order 13636, *Improving Critical Infrastructure Cybersecurity*, February 2013.
http://www.gpo.gov/fdsys/pkg/FR-2013-02-19/pdf/2013-03915.pdf

National Institute of Standards and Technology Federal Information Processing Standards Publication 200 (as amended), *Minimum Security Requirements for Federal Information and Information Systems*.
http://csrc.nist.gov/publications/fips/fips200/FIPS-200-final-march.pdf

National Institute of Standards and Technology Special Publication 800-53 (as amended), *Security and Privacy Controls for Federal Information Systems and Organizations*.
http://dx.doi.org/10.6028/NIST.SP.800-53r4

National Institute of Standards and Technology Special Publication 800-171, rev. 1, *Protecting Controlled Unclassified Information in Nonfederal Information Systems and Organizations*. https://nvlpubs.nist.gov/nistpubs/SpecialPublications/NIST.SP.800-171r1.pdf

National Institute of Standards and Technology Special Publication 800-171A, *Assessing Security Requirements for Controlled Unclassified Information*
https://csrc.nist.gov/CSRC/media/Publications/sp/800-171a/draft/sp800-171A-draft.pdf

National Institute of Standards and Technology *Framework for Improving Critical Infrastructure Cybersecurity* (as amended).
http://www.nist.gov/cyberframework

ANNEX D – Relevant Terms and Glossary

Audit log. A chronological record of information system activities, including records of system accesses and operations performed in a given period.

Authentication. Verifying the identity of a user, process, or device, often as a prerequisite to allowing access to resources in an information system.

Availability. Ensuring timely and reliable access to and use of information.

Baseline Configuration. A documented set of specifications for an information system, or a configuration item within a system, that has been formally reviewed and agreed on at a given point in time, and which can be changed only through change control procedures.

Blacklisting. The process used to identify: (i) software programs that are not authorized to execute on an information system; or (ii) prohibited websites.

Confidentiality. Preserving authorized restrictions on information access and disclosure, including means for protecting personal privacy and proprietary information.

Configuration Management. A collection of activities focused on establishing and maintaining the integrity of information technology products and information systems, through control of processes for initializing, changing, and monitoring the configurations of those products and systems throughout the system development life cycle.

Controlled Unclassified Information (CUI/CDI).

Information that law, regulation, or governmentwide policy requires to have safeguarding or disseminating controls, excluding information that is classified under Executive Order 13526, Classified National Security Information, December 29, 2009, or any predecessor or successor order, or the Atomic Energy Act of 1954, as amended.

FIPS-validated cryptography. A cryptographic module validated by the Cryptographic Module Validation Program (CMVP) to meet requirements specified in FIPS Publication 140-2 (as amended). As a prerequisite to CMVP validation, the cryptographic module is required to employ a cryptographic algorithm implementation that has successfully passed validation testing by the Cryptographic Algorithm Validation Program (CAVP).

Hardware. The physical components of an information system.

Incident. An occurrence that actually or potentially jeopardizes the confidentiality, integrity, or availability of an information system or the information the system processes, stores, or transmits or that constitutes a violation or imminent threat of violation of security policies, security procedures, or acceptable use policies.

Information Security. The protection of information and information systems from unauthorized access, use, disclosure, disruption, modification, or destruction to provide confidentiality, integrity, and availability.

Information System. A discrete set of information resources organized for the collection, processing, maintenance, use, sharing, dissemination, or disposition of information.

Information Technology. Any equipment or interconnected system or subsystem of equipment that is used in the automatic acquisition, storage, manipulation, management, movement, control, display, switching, interchange, transmission, or reception of data or information by the executive agency. It includes computers, ancillary equipment, software, firmware, and similar procedures, services (including support services), and related resources.

Integrity. Guarding against improper information modification or destruction and includes ensuring information non-repudiation and authenticity.

Internal Network. A network where: (i) the establishment, maintenance, and provisioning of security controls are under the direct control of organizational employees or contractors; or (ii) cryptographic encapsulation or similar security technology implemented between organization-controlled endpoints, provides the same effect (at least about confidentiality and integrity).

Malicious Code.	Software intended to perform an unauthorized process that will have adverse impact on the confidentiality, integrity, or availability of an information system. A virus, worm, Trojan horse, or other code-based entity that infects a host. Spyware and some forms of adware are also examples of malicious code.
Media.	Physical devices or writing surfaces including, but not limited to, magnetic tapes, optical disks, magnetic disks, and printouts (but not including display media) onto which information is recorded, stored, or printed within an information system.
Mobile Code.	Software programs or parts of programs obtained from remote information systems, transmitted across a network, and executed on a local information system without explicit installation or execution by the recipient.
Mobile device.	A portable computing device that: (i) has a small form factor such that it can easily be carried by a single individual; (ii) is designed to operate without a physical connection (e.g., wirelessly transmit or receive information); (iii) possesses local, nonremovable or removable data storage; and (iv) includes a self-contained power source. Mobile devices may also include voice communication capabilities, on-board sensors that allow the devices to capture information, and/or built-in features for synchronizing local data with remote locations. Examples include smartphones, tablets, and E-readers.
Multifactor Authentication.	Authentication using two or more different factors to achieve authentication. Factors include: (i) something you know (e.g., password/PIN); (ii) something you have (e.g., cryptographic identification device, token); or (iii) something you are (e.g., biometric).
Nonfederal Information System.	An information system that does not meet the criteria for a federal information system. nonfederal organization.
Network.	Information system(s) implemented with a collection of interconnected components. Such components may include routers, hubs, cabling, telecommunications controllers, key distribution centers, and technical control devices.

Portable storage device.	An information system component that can be inserted into and removed from an information system, and that is used to store data or information (e.g., text, video, audio, and/or image data). Such components are typically implemented on magnetic, optical, or solid-state devices (e.g., floppy disks, compact/digital video disks, flash/thumb drives, external hard disk drives, and flash memory cards/drives that contain nonvolatile memory).
Privileged Account. user.	An information system account with authorizations of a privileged
Privileged User.	A user that is authorized (and therefore, trusted) to perform security-relevant functions that ordinary users are not authorized to perform.
Remote Access.	Access to an organizational information system by a user (or a process acting on behalf of a user) communicating through an external network (e.g., the Internet).
Risk.	A measure of the extent to which an entity is threatened by a potential circumstance or event, and typically a function of: (i) the adverse impacts that would arise if the circumstance or event occurs; and (ii) the likelihood of occurrence. Information system-related security risks are those risks that arise from the loss of confidentiality, integrity, or availability of information or information systems and reflect the potential adverse impacts to organizational operations (including mission, functions, image, or reputation), organizational assets, individuals, other organizations, and the Nation.
Sanitization.	Actions taken to render data written on media unrecoverable by both ordinary and, for some forms of sanitization, extraordinary means. Process to remove information from media such that data recovery is not possible. It includes removing all classified labels, markings, and activity logs.
Security Control.	A safeguard or countermeasure prescribed for an information system or an organization designed to protect the confidentiality,

integrity, and availability of its information and to meet a set of defined security requirements.

Security Control Assessment.   The testing or evaluation of security controls to determine the extent to which the controls are implemented correctly, operating as intended, and producing the desired outcome with respect to meeting the security requirements for an information system or organization.

Security Functions.   The hardware, software, and/or firmware of the information system responsible for enforcing the system security policy and supporting the isolation of code and data on which the protection is based.

Threat.   Any circumstance or event with the potential to adversely impact organizational operations (including mission, functions, image, or reputation), organizational assets, individuals, other organizations, or the Nation through an information system via unauthorized access, destruction, disclosure, modification of information, and/or denial of service.

Whitelisting.   The process used to identify: (i) software programs that are authorized to execute on an information system.

About the Author

Mr. Russo is a former Senior Information Security Engineer within the Department of Defense's (DOD) F-35 Joint Strike Fighter program. He has an extensive background in cybersecurity and is an expert in the Risk Management Framework (RMF) to include DOD Instruction (DODI) 8510.01 which implements RMF throughout the DOD and the federal government. He holds both a Certified Information Systems Security Professional (CISSP) certification and a CISSP in information security architecture (ISSAP). He holds a 2017 certification as a Chief Information Security Officer (CISO) from the National Defense University, Washington, DC. He retired from the US Army Reserves in 2012 as the Senior Intelligence Officer.

He is the former CISO at the Department of Education wherein 2016 he led the effort to close over 95% of the outstanding US Congressional and Inspector General cybersecurity shortfall weaknesses spanning as far back as five years.

Mr. Russo is the former Senior Cybersecurity Engineer supporting the Joint Medical Logistics Development Functional Center of the Defense Health Agency (DHA) at Fort Detrick, MD. He led a team of engineering and cybersecurity professionals protecting five major Medical Logistics systems supporting over 200 DOD Medical Treatment Facilities around the globe.

In 2011, Mr. Russo was certified by the Office of Personnel Management as a graduate of the Senior Executive Service Candidate program.

From 2009 through 2011, Mr. Russo was the Chief Technology Officer at the Small Business Administration (SBA). He led a team of over 100 IT professionals in supporting an intercontinental Enterprise IT infrastructure and security operations spanning 12-time zones; he deployed cutting-edge technologies to enhance SBA's business and information sharing operations supporting the small business community. Mr. Russo was the first-ever Program Executive Officer (PEO)/Senior Program Manager in the Office of Intelligence & Analysis at Headquarters, Department of Homeland Security (DHS), Washington, DC. Mr. Russo was responsible for the development and deployment of secure Information and Intelligence support systems for OI&A to include software applications and systems to enhance the DHS mission. He was responsible for the program management development lifecycle during his tenure at DHS.

He holds a Master of Science from the National Defense University in Government Information Leadership with a concentration in Cybersecurity and a Bachelor of Arts in Political Science with a minor in Russian Studies from Lehigh University. He holds Level III Defense Acquisition certification in Program Management, Information Technology, and Systems Engineering. He has been a member of the DOD Acquisition Corps since 2001.

Check out these latest Cybersecurity Books at Amazon by the Author

Agile/Security Development Life Cycle (A/SDLC): Integrating Security into the System Development Life Cycle

https://www.amazon.com/Agile-Security-Development-Cycle-ASDLC-ebook/dp/B07GLBYZVT/ref=sr_1_1?ie=UTF8&qid=1536968618&sr=8-1&keywords=Agile+cybersecurity

THE AGILE/SECURITY DEVELOPMENT LIFE CYCLE (ASDLC) is a book designed to address the ongoing shortfalls and failures of "Secure System Development." The author seeks to use his over 20 years in the public and private sector program management and cybersecurity to create a solution. This book provides the first-ever integrated operational-security process to enhance the readers understanding of why systems are so poorly secured. Why we as a nation have missed the mark in cybersecurity? Why nation-states and hackers are successful daily? This book also describes the two major mainstream "agile" NIST frameworks that can be employed, and how to use them effectively under a Risk Management approach. We may be losing "battles, " but may be its time we truly commit to winning this cyber-war.

The Threat Hunting Process (THP) Roadmap: A Pathway for Advanced Cybersecurity Active Measures

https://www.amazon.com/Threat-Hunting-Process-Roadmap-Cybersecurity-ebook/dp/B07MKJJ99Z/ref=sr_1_1?ie=UTF8&qid=1545954680&sr=8-1&keywords=threat+hunting+process

This book is designed to implement the most extensive Threat Hunt Process (THP) for companies and agencies seeking to proactively determine whether intrusions into their Information Technology (IT) environments is real and malicious. THP is the active ability for businesses or organizations to investigate, mitigate, and stop the "bad guys" in their tracks. How do you select, collect, align, and integrate THP data and information for tracking daily operations and overall organizational security? How do you reduce the effort in THP activities to get problems solved? How can you ensure that plans include every THP task and that every possibility is considered and responded to by the Incident Response Team? How can you save time investigating and responding to strategic and tactical threats with limited resources? This book is designed to help you create an effective and repeatable THP.

From the best-selling Cybersecurity author, Mr. Mark A. Russo, holds multiple cybersecurity certifications from several international bodies to include the International Information System Security Certification Consortium, (ISC2), the premier certification body for cybersecurity, and the International Council of Electronic Commerce Consultants (EC Council). Mr. Russo has extensive experience applying cybersecurity and threat intelligence expertise for over 20 years as a retired intelligence officer from the United States Army.

www.ingramcontent.com/pod-product-compliance
Lightning Source LLC
Chambersburg PA
CBHW070846070326
40690CB00009B/1719